Backyard Animals
Deer

Christine Webster

Weigl Publishers Inc.

Published by Weigl Publishers Inc.
350 5th Avenue, Suite 3304, PMB 6G
New York, NY 10118-0069
Website: www.weigl.com

Library of Congress Cataloging-in-Publication Data

Webster, Christine.
  Deer / Christine Webster.
      p. cm. -- (Backyard animals)
  Includes index.
  ISBN 978-1-59036-675-2 (hard cover : alk. paper) -- ISBN 978-1-59036-676-9 (soft
cover : alk. paper)
  1. Deer--Juvenile literature. I. Title.
  QL737.U55W38 2008
  599.65--dc22
                                        2006102087

Printed in the United States of America
1 2 3 4 5 6 7 8 9 0 11 10 09 08 07

Editor Heather C. Hudak
Design and Layout Terry Paulhus

Cover: Deer spend most of their lives searching for food.

Contents

Meet the Deer

Deer are **mammals**. They have big eyes and sharp hearing. Deer have a keen sense of smell. They can run very fast, and they are good swimmers.

Deer are covered with fur. The fur is usually reddish-brown in the summer. It is grayish in the winter. These colors let a deer easily blend into its surroundings. This helps the deer to hide from **predators**.

Male deer are called bucks. Bucks have **antlers** on their head. Most female deer do not have antlers. They are called does.

Deer are found in North America, Europe, northern Africa, and Asia. They live in open meadows, mountains, forests, and swamps.

Most deer have a gland in front of each eye. They use this to spray a smelly scent where they live and eat.

Deer can run as fast as 36 miles (58 kilometers) per hour.

All about Deer

There are more than 30 deer **species**. Each species has special features. Deer are the only animals with antlers on their head.

Some deer species, such as the Chinese water deer, are very small. The smallest deer is the South American pudu. It is only 10 inches (25 centimeters) high at the shoulder. Other species, such as the moose, are quite big.

Often, only male deer grow antlers. In some species, such as caribou, both males and females grow antlers.

Sizes of Deer

American Elk	Caribou	Chinese Water Deer
• Weighs 650 pounds (295 kilograms) to 1,000 pounds (454 kg)	• Males weigh 275 pounds (125 kg) to 660 pounds (300 kg)	• Weight ranges from 200 pounds (91 kg) to 300 pounds (136 kg)

Moose	Mule Deer	White-tailed Deer
• Largest member of the deer family • Males can weigh up to 1,800 pounds (816 kg)	• Weighs 110 pounds (50 kg) to 475 pounds (215 kg)	• Weighs 150 to 300 pounds (68 to 136 kg)

Deer History

Deer have been on Earth for millions of years. The first deer appeared in Asia about 38 million years ago. Scientists believe that deer once lived only in Arctic areas. They began living in parts of North America about 4 million years ago.

At one time, the deer's biggest threats were predators. These include wolves and mountain lions. Humans also hunted deer as a food source.

Today, humans are the deer's main predator. Humans hunt deer for many reasons. Deer are hunted for their meat, or venison. Their skin can be used as clothing.

Fascinating Facts

The Irish elk has not lived on Earth since 5000 B.C. This giant animal stood 7 feet (2.1 m) at the shoulder. Its antlers measured more than 12 feet (3.7 m) across.

Mule deer are sometimes called
black-tailed deer. This is because
they have a black-tipped tail.

Deer Shelter

Most deer live in forests or near grassy meadows. They rest on the ground. The place where they rest is called a deer bed. Deer look for places that are surrounded by tall grasses, plants, trees, and shrubs. This protects them from harsh weather, such as rain or snow. It also hides them from predators. A deer bed is about 4 feet (1.2 m) long and 1.5 feet (0.5 m) wide.

Male deer mark their territory by stomping on the ground and making scrape marks in the dirt. They may rub their antlers on trees. This is called a buck rub.

Some deer, such as caribou, travel from place to place with the changing seasons. This is called migration.

Some species of deer live in forests. Others live near water.

Deer Features

A deer's body is adapted to offer protection from predators. Strong legs allow deer to leap 9-foot (2.7-m) fences. They can swim 13 miles (21 km) per hour. The color of their fur helps deer hide well in forests. Every part of a deer's body is finely tuned with special uses.

EYES
Deer have large eyes on both sides of their head. This allows them to see in front and behind without moving their head.

NOSE
A deer's sense of smell is much more sensitive than a human's. A deer's nose has membranes that capture scents easily. Membranes are thin layers of skin tissue.

TEETH
Deer teeth are made to chew tough food, such as plants. Deer have **incisors** that allow them to bite. **Molars** help deer grind their food into smaller pieces.

EARS
Deer have large ears. They can hear very well. Deer ears rotate, or turn, acting like **radar**. They pick up sounds quickly.

COAT
A deer's coat acts as **camouflage.** It is reddish-brown in the summer to blend in with the leaves on trees. It is grayish-brown in the winter, so it blends in with the bare forests.

What Do Deer Eat?

Deer are herbivores. This means they eat plants, such as herbs, leaves, and grass. Deer choose foods that can be easily **digested**. In the summer, they graze on leaves, grass, alfalfa, wheat, berries, acorns, and herbs. During the winter, deer eat twigs, wildflowers, nuts, and fruits. They will **scavenge** corn, wheat, and soybeans from farmers' fields.

A deer's stomach has four chambers to help digest this food more easily. In the first chamber, acids break down the tough plant fibers. Later, the deer will cough up the food. The deer re-chews and swallows the food. It then passes through the other three stomach chambers.

Fascinating Facts

Scientists can tell the age of a deer by looking at its teeth. This is because deer's teeth become shorter each year. Older deer will have shorter teeth.

Deer are often fearful of predators. This causes them to eat their food quickly.

Deer Life Cycle

The deer's mating season is called a rut. Bucks will fight for their territory during this time. A male will crash his antlers against another male to claim a female.

Birth

At birth, a white-tailed fawn has a reddish coat with white spots. It weighs 3 pounds (1.4 kg) to 7 pounds (3.2 kg). Shortly after birth, the doe quickly licks the fawn clean. This is so predators do not smell its scent. Fawns take a step within 20 minutes after being born.

1 Day to 5 Months

The mother hides the fawn in the grass for one week. This allows the baby time to grow strong. During this time, the fawn nibbles on plants and drinks its mother's milk. At 6 weeks, fawns stop drinking their mother's milk. Their spots fade after about five months.

A doe is pregnant for five to ten months. Does give birth in May or June. Baby deer are called fawns or calves. A doe can have one to three fawns.

Adult

Female fawns may stay with their mother for two years. Males often leave after a year. At this time, they are considered to be adults. They are ready to live on their own.

Encountering Deer

Often a doe will leave her fawns for hours at a time while she finds food. Most times, she will return. A doe will not come for her fawn if a human is nearby. It is best to leave the area without touching the fawn.

If a fawn is injured or ill, call a wildlife officer for help. The fawn may need to be moved to a safe place. Ask an adult to gently put the animal in a cardboard box. Pad the box with towels and blankets. The fawn may be scared and upset. It is important not to touch or talk to the fawn. The fawn can have water to drink. Do not give it food. The wildlife officer will know how to help the fawn.

Useful Websites

To learn more about caring for deer, check out
www.worldalmanacforkids.com/ explore/animals/deer.html

People often see deer while hiking through natural areas. Hikers should not feed or touch the animals.

Myths and Legends

People all over the world have myths about deer. Deer are very important to the Huichol people of Mexico. They believe the deer is the symbol of Kayumahli. He is a guide and guardian that only shamans can hear. Shamans are spiritual guides.

The Huichol believed their ancestors came from wolves. The Huichol would hunt deer and offer the animal's blood to the gods or goddesses. This allowed the Huichol to remain human.

In the city of Nara, people believed deer were messengers of the gods. Today, deer can be found in Nara Deer Park, in southern Honshu, Japan.

How the Deer Got His Antlers

Here is a retold legend passed down by Cherokee Indians.

Deer had no antlers, but he was a fast runner. His friend Rabbit was a great jumper. The animals in the forest wanted to know who could travel the fastest. Rabbit and Deer agreed to race. The winner would receive a pair of antlers.

Rabbit and Deer were to race through a thicket, turn, and come back. Before they began, Rabbit said, "I don't know this part of the country. I want to take a look through the bushes to see where to run."

Rabbit went into the thicket. He was gone so long that the other animals became worried. They sent someone to look for him. Rabbit was found gnawing on bushes to clear a path. The messenger told the other animals. Rabbit was accused of cheating. They gave the antlers to Deer. He has worn them ever since.

Frequently Asked Questions

Do deer grow new antlers each year?

Answer: Bucks shed their antlers each year. They grow new antlers in the summer. If they have plenty of healthy food, their antlers will grow bigger each year.

What do deer tracks look like?

Answer: Deer have hoofs. These are like toenails. Hoofs make a heart-shaped track on the ground. The pointed part of a track shows which way a deer is traveling.

What do deer sound like?

Answer: Deer make many sounds. A white-tailed fawn looking for its mother will bleat like a sheep. An injured white-tailed deer will bawl. This is a long, loud, high-pitched call. All deer make a snorting sound.

Puzzler

See how much you know about deer.

1. How many deer species are there?
2. Why does a mother deer hide its baby for a week?
3. Where do deer live?
4. How high can a deer jump?
5. What do deer eat?

Answers: 1. more than 30 2. to allow the fawn to gain strength 3. forests, open meadows, mountains, and swamps 4. 9 feet (2.7 m) 5. leaves, grass, alfalfa, wheat, berries, acorns, herbs, twigs, wildflowers, nuts, and fruits

Find Out More

There are many more interesting facts to learn about deer. If you would like to learn more, look for these books at your library.

Evert, Laura. *Whitetail Deer*. Northword Press, 2000.

Rue, Leonard Lee. *The Encyclopedia of Deer*. Voyageur Press, 2004.

Words to Know

antlers: bony growths on a deer's head

camouflage: to blend in

digested: to be broken down in the stomach into substances that can be used by the body

incisors: front teeth used for cutting and gnawing

mammals: any warm-blooded animals born with a backbone that drink their mother's milk

molars: back teeth that have a broad biting surface

predators: animals that hunt other animals for food

radar: an instrument that bounces radio waves off unseen objects to find out where they are located, how fast they are moving, and in what direction they are traveling

scavenge: to take something usable from discarded material

species: animals or plants that share certain features

Index